That is my cap.

My cap has a flap.

My cap is in my lap...

as I nap.

Tap, tap, tap!

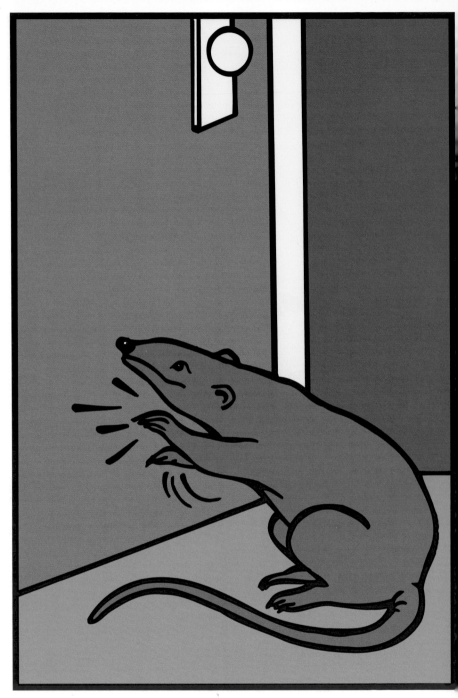

Rap, rap, rap!

Slap, slap, slap!

A bat, a rat, and a cat
did that!

No nap!

No cap!

"Do not slap my cap
from my lap!"

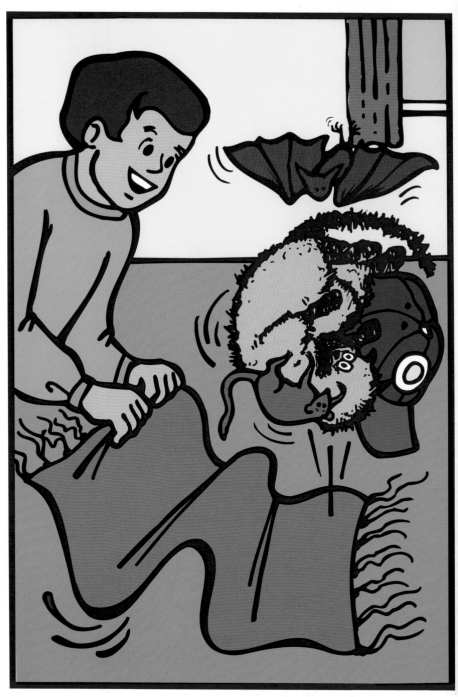

I will grab that mat!

Splat!

The bat, the rat, and
the cat...

sat on my hat.

My hat is flat!